THE STORY OF
FORD

L O N N I E   B E L L

A⁺

Published by Smart Apple Media
1980 Lookout Drive, North Mankato, Minnesota 56003

Photographs by Corbis (Robert Holmes, Bo Zaunders), Richard Cummins, Ford
Motor Company, Alan Look, Time Life Pictures/Getty Images (Frank Scherschel)

Library of Congress Cataloging-in-Publication Data
Bell, Lonnie.
The story of Ford / by Lonnie Bell.
p. cm. — (Built for success)
Summary: Describes the founding and development of the Ford
Motor Company, makers of the first affordable family cars.
Includes bibliographical references.
ISBN 1-58340-293-4
1. Ford Motor Company—History—Juvenile literature. 2. Automobile
industry and trade—United States—History—Juvenile literature.
[1. Ford Motor Company—History.] I. Title. II. Series.
HD9710.U54 F5339 2003
338.7'6292'0973—dc21
2002036569

First Edition
2 4 6 8 9 7 5 3 1

THE STORY OF
FORD

Table of Contents

Building a Dream

In many ways, the story of Henry Ford is the story of the Ford Motor Company. From the rainy night in 1896 when he took his first vehicle for a spin until the day he died, Ford and the company he founded were tightly woven together.

The Ford Motor Company had 345,000 employees and 13,000 dealers in 125 countries across six continents in 2003. Ford's blue oval is the second most recognized symbol in the world. That's pretty amazing, considering that Henry Ford began with less than a dollar in his pocket.

Henry Ford, a farmer's son, wasn't much of a farmer but he loved machines. "Henry's a **tinkerer**," his father often said. In 1879, when he was 17 years old, Henry walked for half a day to Detroit, Michigan, and took a job in a machine shop. Over the next few years, he changed jobs several times. Then one day when he was repairing and demonstrating steam engines, he saw an internal combustion engine for the first time. Henry went home and said to his wife, Clara, "What I would like to do is make an engine that will run by gasoline and have it do the work of a horse."

Henry Ford wasn't the first person to have such a crazy idea. A Frenchman built what was probably the first automobile in 1769. The steam car went two miles (3.2 km) per hour and stopped every 20 minutes when it ran out of steam. For the next 100 years, other inventors experimented with electric and even kerosene engines. In 1876, a German named Nikolaus August Otto created a gasoline-powered engine. Nine years later, another German, Gottlieb Daimler, improved the engine and attached it to a bicycle. In 1893, Charles Duryea built a successful gasoline motorcar in the United States.

Henry Ford was a pioneer of the automobile industry

Henry built an internal combustion engine from plans he saw in a magazine. In 1896, he mounted his engine on bicycle wheels with a boat tiller to steer. He called the vehicle a Quadricycle because it had four wheels.

At 2:00 A.M. on June 4, 1896, Henry got ready to drive the Quadricycle for the first time. But the **chassis** was too big to fit through the doors of his machine shop. He grabbed an ax, knocked a hole in the wall, and drove through it. Henry later recalled, "The motor roared and sputtered to life. The car bumped along the cobblestones of the alley." One of Henry's friends rode ahead on a bicycle to warn any horse-drawn vehicles he was coming.

Henry sold that first automobile for $200 and used the money to begin work on a new vehicle. By then he was working for the Detroit Automobile Company. But he was not happy with the expensive cars the company was making. He wanted to make a cheaper car for ordinary working people. However, he needed cash.

In 1901, Henry began racing cars to show off his designs to wealthy people. In his first race, he wowed the

The Quadricycle looked like a buggy without a horse

For Edsel Ford
from his friend
... Roosevelt

crowd by beating racing celebrity Alexander Winton and winning the $1,000 prize. Henry kept racing and winning, and word soon spread about his remarkable vehicles.

On June 17, 1903, Henry and 11 financial **backers** founded the Ford Motor Company with $28,000. A local reporter wrote, "Mr. Ford's name has hitherto been connected with his fast speed freaks, but he is preparing to put a 'family horse' on the market." One month after Ford opened, the company sold its first Model A for $850. Over the next 15 months, the company sold an amazing 1,700 cars. In 1904, Ford Motor

President Franklin Delano Roosevelt drove a Model A

Company of Canada opened for business. In 1911, the first overseas plant was established in England. Two years later, Ford had assembly plants throughout the world.

When Henry began the Ford Motor Company, there were more than 2,000 steam, electric, and gasoline automobiles in U.S. cities. More than 100 companies were in the automobile-making business. Most were failing, in part because of legal battles with George B. Selden. Selden had seen a gasoline engine at the Philadelphia Centennial Exposition in 1876. He designed a similar engine and obtained a **patent** for all "road locomotives" powered by internal combustion engines. Selden did not manufacture the engines or automobiles; he just collected **royalties** from those who did. Henry refused to

By 1905, there were more than 450 Ford dealerships

pay him. After eight years, the courts ruled that Selden's patent applied only to two-stroke engines. Henry was using a four-stroke engine.

Everything seemed to be coming together for Henry Ford. First, a lightweight steel was developed in Britain that was nearly three times stronger than American steel. By the turn of the century it was being made in the United States, and Henry planned to use it to make his autos.

Secondly, oil had been discovered outside Beaumont, Texas. Henry planned to build a car that everyone could afford to buy, but the oil needed to run a car was so expensive that only rich Americans could afford it. At the time, most U.S. oil was produced on the East Coast. No one believed there was any oil in Texas, except one man named Patillo Higgins. For years, he had watched children drop lighted matches in a field near Beaumont. The matches hit petroleum vapors hovering above the soil and caused small explosions. Higgins kept drilling until 1901, when a geyser of oil finally gushed out of the ground. Soon, Texas oil wells were producing 60 percent of America's oil. There was lots of it, and it was cheap!

Oil pumps quickly became a familiar sight in Texas

Finally, Henry found a way to make cars quickly and thus cheaply. In 1906, he offered $20,000 to Walter Flanders if the factory expert could produce 10,000 cars in just 12 months. Flanders reorganized Ford's factory and beat the deadline by two days.

Model As were built one at a time by teams of mechanics

Better, Faster, Cheaper

By 1908, the stage was set. Henry began production of the Model T. "I will build a car for the multitude," he said. "It will be so low in price that no man making a good salary will be unable to own one." The T was tough, light, and simple. Most of the roads that existed at the time were unimproved horse trails, but the T chugged easily over them. There was just one problem: Ford had a tough time keeping up with all the orders.

In 1910, Henry opened a plant in Highland Park, Michigan, where he planned to use modern production techniques. By 1913, he was experimenting with assembly-line manufacturing. "The way to make automobiles," he told his backers, "is to make one automobile like another automobile . . . just as one pin is like another pin when it comes from a pin factory."

At the time, skilled mechanics were building engines one at a time. Henry and factory expert Frederick Winslow Taylor broke down each engine-building task into smaller tasks. For instance, it took one man 20 minutes and 29 different tasks to build the **magneto**. Taylor sat the workers side-by-side at a table. Each worker performed one or two tasks

The Model T came in "any color as long as it's black"

and then gave the part to the next worker. Using this system, they could build a magneto seven minutes faster.

Over the next year, Henry and Charles Sorenson, another factory expert, improved the assembly line. Sorenson rigged up a system to pull a Model T chassis across the factory floor. Six workers walked behind it picking up car parts from piles on the floor and fitting them to the chassis. Following that experiment, the company installed its first automatic conveyor belt. Now, instead of moving with the car, workers stayed in one place and put the parts on the chassis as it slowly moved along the belt.

When Henry began producing the Model T in 1908, it took more than 12 hours to make one car. Less than 12 years later, he was making one car every minute. Five years later, he

Wheeling and Dealing

For 100 years, Ford has had a special relationship with the dealers who sell the company's vehicles. Many of Ford's first dealers were young men with a sense of adventure. Selling automobiles could be very difficult. No one knew if the "crazy fad" was going to last. Dealers set up business on the sidewalk and worked hard to make a sale. Customers often bet with them: "If you can make it up that hill in high gear, I'll buy the car." The Model T usually won that wager!

Once the car was sold, dealers had to be prepared to teach people how to drive and pump gas. They even taught some rural customers how to read so they could pass the test to get a driver's license.

was making one T every 10 seconds. "Watch the Fords roll by!" proclaimed a sign outside the factory. Once Henry could **mass produce** cars, he cut prices from $780 in 1910 to a low in 1925 of $290—about nine weeks' wages for a skilled manual laborer. Later in life, Henry was arguing with a boy who had become frustrated with Henry's narrow point of view. "But sir," said the boy, "these are different times, this is the modern age...." Henry interrupted him: "Young man, I invented the modern age."

In 1915, Henry purchased several acres of property alongside the river Rouge outside Dearborn, Michigan, where he planned to develop industrial buildings for making steel, manufacturing parts, and assembling automobiles. Construction began on the Rouge plant in 1917. By the late 1920s, it covered more than 150 acres (60 ha). It encompassed 90 structures, more than 90 miles (145 km) of railroad tracks, and 27 miles (44 km) of conveyor belts. The plant employed more than 100,000 workers. Much like a city, the Rouge had its own fire station, security force, hospital, schools, and dining facilities. Buses and streetcars transported workers to their jobs from company housing.

Above, Ford was proud of its contribution to the war effort;
below, jeeps and bombers were assembled at Willow Run

The Rouge plant was also environmentally friendly. Ore dust from the blast furnaces was captured and melted down. Oven gases were trapped and reused as additional sources of power.

No one had ever seen anything like the Rouge. But workers were not entirely happy with the new plant and its assembly-line system. Skilled men, who once had been proud to build a car from the ground up, were bored. They now spent all day doing one or two tasks over and over again. The day the Rouge opened, workers streamed out of the plant. The employee **turnover** in 1913 was 380 percent. In 1914, Henry tried to stop the flow of employees. He began offering workers $5.00 a day. The national average was $2.40 a day. More than 10,000 men turned up at the gates looking for work, including some of Detroit's most skilled mechanics.

The last assembly line at Highland Park moved to the Rouge in 1927. During World War II, the plant stopped car production and made tank parts, aircraft engines, and parts for bombers. The bomber parts were shipped to Ford's plant in Willow Run, Michigan. There, Ford assembled more than

8,000 planes, 57,000 aircraft engines, and 250,000 tanks, jeeps, and other equipment for the war. After World War II ended, the Rouge went back to making trucks, cars, jeeps, and tractors. With every vehicle they made, workers got better and faster. They often broke their own performance records. But during the 1950s, U.S. factories changed. The Rouge had been supplying parts to factories all around the country, but now many Ford plants were buying materials from local suppliers. Activity slowed at the Rouge plant, and by 1992, only one car, the Mustang, was manufactured there.

The Rouge plant represented a new approach to industry

Motoring through Tough Times

As the Ford Motor Company grew, Henry's **stockholders** wanted to make fancier, more expensive cars. Henry believed he had built the only car anyone would ever need when he built the Model T. Rather than design new vehicles, he wanted to put money back into the company to make it bigger. Henry and his son, Edsel, bought up all the stockholders' **shares**. The Ford family maintained complete control over the company from 1919 to 1956.

Edsel was the only child of Henry and Clara Ford

Edsel was named company president in 1919. Edsel was not a mechanical man, but he was a good businessman with an eye for design. "Father made the most popular car in the world," he said. "I would like to make the best car in the world."

In 1922, the company's sales were higher than ever. But as roads improved, other companies were building faster, more comfortable vehicles. Ford's executives and the dealers who sold his cars begged Henry to change the Model T. People even began laughing at the once beloved automobile and calling it the "Tin Lizzie." One joke asked, "What does the Model T use for **shock absorbers**?" The reply: "The passengers."

Edsel urged Henry to update the Model T, but Henry rejected his son's advice. When Ford sales dropped from $1.87 million to $1.67 million in 1926, Henry finally announced that he would build a new car. On the day the new Model A was unveiled, crowds flocked to showplaces in Detroit to see it. The car had shock absorbers, a standard gearshift, gas gauge, and speedometer. Before it was on the market, dealers had 727,000 orders. After he introduced the new Model A, however, Henry refused to update it.

More than 4.5 million new Model As were produced

Over the years, Edsel made some progress. He convinced Henry to buy the Lincoln Motor Company in 1922 so Ford could compete with Cadillac. In 1933, Edsel introduced the company's first design department. About the same time, Ford developed the V-8 engine, which had eight cylinders instead of four. The powerful engine was well received and is still used today.

A Burning Question

How does the internal combustion engine work? A mixture of gas and air is burned inside a closed cylinder, or tube. Inside the cylinder is a **piston** that slides. Each piston movement is called a stroke. In a four-stroke engine, the piston moves four times:

1) The driver steps on the gas pedal, and gasoline is pumped from the fuel tank to the engine. It mixes with air and becomes a vapor. An intake valve opens at the top of a cylinder, and the vapor is sucked in.

2) The valve closes, and the piston moves up, heating and compressing, or squashing, the vapor. The hot gas reaches the top of the cylinder.

3) An electric spark plug fires. The spark lights the vapor, causing a small explosion that pushes the piston down. When a car is running, there are hundreds of explosions every minute.

4) An outlet valve opens, and the piston moves up, pushing exhaust gases out of the cylinder.

As the piston moves up and down, it turns a rotating device called the crankshaft, which is linked to the driveshaft that turns the car wheels.

Most engines have four cylinders. A V-8 engine has eight cylinders, all of which spark and move at the same time for a powerful and smooth ride.

ANNOUNCING THE NEW FORD V-8 Cylinder

THE NEW FORD EIGHT *De Luxe Tudor Sedan*

Sadly, many of the company's changes came too late. From 1930 to 1936, automobiles became luxurious and visually appealing. They featured strong braking systems and powerful engines. General Motors Corporation (GMC) had spent years modernizing its design, production, and marketing. It was beating Ford sales year after year.

Ford was having other troubles as well. **Labor unions** were trying to organize auto industry workers. Henry did not want labor unions interfering with his company. In 1935, the National Labor Relations Board ruled that the Ford Company

Ford was the first company to mass-produce V-8 engines

Henry's Fair Lane estate was built in Dearborn, Michigan, in 1915

had repeatedly violated the Wagner Act, which stated that workers had the right to **bargain** as a group for fair wages and better treatment. In 1937, union organizers began passing out flyers at the gates of the Rouge plant. The flyers told employees about worker rights. Henry's men attacked the union people. Reporters published photographs of the brutal battle. The workers went on **strike**, and Ford was forced to negotiate a **labor contract**. Since then, Ford's relationship with the unions has strengthened and improved.

When Edsel died at age 49 in 1943, Henry's wife, Clara, and Edsel's widow, Eleanor, wanted to make sure that Edsel's son, Henry II, would head up the struggling company. They said they would sell their company stock if Henry didn't step down. Henry's 28-year-old grandson finally took control in 1945. The change came just in time; the company was losing an estimated $10 million every month.

Two years later, 83-year-old Henry died at Fair Lane, his 56-room mansion. It had been an amazing career. In 1947, he was worth $600 million. He had sold 15,456,868 Model Ts and forever changed the way America did business.

The 1949 Ford wagon featured luxuries such as wood paneling

A New Era Dawns

Henry Ford II ushered in the modern era at Ford. He surrounded himself with managers who were so skilled at running a business that they became known as "Whiz Kids." Ford began to make sleek, refined cars featuring fenders molded into the bodywork, sealed-beam headlights, and automatic transmissions. The futuristic 1949 Ford was a landmark design. In the first year, the company sold 87,000 models—the most since the Model A was introduced. It ensured the company's survival.

During the 1950s, designers borrowed outrageous designs, such as tailfins and portholes, from aircraft and ships. Air conditioning and electrical windows and seat adjusters were introduced. As vehicles got fancier, Ford faced a lingering problem. Consumers had come to think of Ford as the low-priced car that young people bought when they didn't have much money. As people became wealthier, they bought GMC cars. Ford countered the image problem with its first luxury cars—the Thunderbird and Fairlane.

When Ford unveiled the Edsel in 1958, there were few buyers. The grille was compared to an Oldsmobile sucking a

lemon. Only 84,000 were made, and the car was discontinued in 1959. Today, the car is considered a collectible, but at the time it was viewed as ridiculous. The press also laughed in 1960 when Ford introduced the plain little Falcon. They called it a "modern version of the Tin Lizzie." But this time, the reporters were wrong. Money was tight, and the average American loved the economical car. Ford sold more than 400,000 cars in the first year.

In 1956, Ford's stock went up for public sale. By the end of the day on January 17, 10.2 million shares had been

The Edsel was designed to be recognizable from any angle

Above, the Mustang was named for a World War II fighter plane;
below, the 1955 Thunderbird was the first personal luxury car

sold. People outside of the family now owned 22 percent of the business.

By the 1960s, American cars were smaller, but they had larger engines and more horsepower. Some of the gas-guzzlers made only eight miles (13 km) to the gallon (3.8 l). In 1961, Ford introduced its own powerful car. It jazzed up the Falcon's interior and reintroduced it as the Mustang. When one product planner saw the car at the test track, he exclaimed, "This car collects crowds." The Mustang made Ford look hip and up-to-date. But at heart it was still a simple, tough, afford-able Ford. Young buyers loved it. The first day on the market, Ford had 22,000 orders. By 1970, the Ford Motor Company was three times larger than the company Henry II had inherit-ed. It was doing $15 billion in sales, much of it overseas.

When environmental pollution became a growing con-cern, compact cars and devices to reduce pollution were intro-duced. Henry II was ready. "We are convinced that the switch to smaller cars is . . . a permanent feature of the American car markets," he said. The little Pinto seemed just right for the times. But the company was turned upside down when rear-end collisions caused Pinto fuel tanks to explode. Many people filed lawsuits. Henry Ford II stoically took the blame. In 1979, he retired, saying, "After 34 years on the job, I am ready to stand aside."

As a toddler, Henry Ford II had pushed the button that started production at the Rouge. Upon his retirement, he had been head of a major corporation longer than any other person in the history of American industry. His successor, Philip Caldwell, became the first person outside the Ford family to lead the company.

In 1985, Ford introduced the sleek Taurus. It was named the best American car, and Ford beat GMC sales for the first time since 1926. Ford's new slogan, "Have you driven a Ford lately," suggested that customers were in for a nice sur-

Recycling the Rouge

In 1997, Ford decided to preserve its unique industrial history for future generations. It announced a plan to recycle the Rouge complex. When the Rouge Center is complete, its body shop and assembly plant will occupy 1.7 million square feet (157,935 sq m). There will be a training center, day care center, and stores.

The Rouge Center will also feature a living roof of plants that soak up runoff storm water, shade the building, and absorb harmful greenhouse gases. Porous parking lot surfaces will absorb water, and extra runoff will be filtered for pollutants before it flows back to the river.

In the future, other Ford work sites will be modeled after the plant.

prise. Drivers seemed to agree. In 1987, the company made a record $4.63 billion. In the '90s, Ford made five of the eight best-selling vehicles in America. The company that had offered the first factory-installed seat belts now introduced the Beltminder, a device with chimes and lights that encouraged drivers to buckle up.

Ford produced 7.4 million vehicles in 2000. But the company hit another roadblock when **tire tread** on Ford Explorers split apart, causing rollover accidents. After the dust cleared, the public agreed with Ford that the blame lay with Firestone, the tire company. But both companies suffered. Ford's sales and revenues in 2001 were $162 billion, down from $170 billion in 2000.

Ford asked customers for input when designing the Taurus

100 Years and Growing Strong

By 2002, Ford was recovering its strength. The Ford Focus was the best-selling car in the world. The Ford F-series were the best-selling trucks. Ford planned to introduce new products such as the Cross-Trainer, which combines the family car with a sport-utility vehicle. It created the first side air-curtain to protect people in rollover accidents and was developing a pre-crash sensing device to predict accidents.

On the eve of its 100th anniversary, Ford's family of brands included Lincoln, Volvo, Jaguar, Land Rover, Aston Martin, Mercury, and Mazda. Ford also held interests in financial services, car rentals, and the air and space industries.

In addition to its contributions to industry and technology, the Ford Motor Company has made many contributions to society. In 1936, Henry and Edsel Ford founded the Ford Foundation, which has provided more than $12 billion over the years to reduce poverty and injustice, promote democracy and peace, and support human achievement. Following the 1967 race riots in Detroit, Henry Ford II expanded Ford's minority hiring program and created minor-

Today, the Ford Foundation is independent from the company

36

Battery-operated TH!NK cars have a range of about 50 miles (80.5 km)

ity dealer and supplier development programs. These programs served as models for similar programs in other U.S. companies. Ford has also focused on solving environmental concerns. In 2001, its P2000 fuel cell vehicle set a 24-hour world record for speed and distance. It used no gasoline and produced no emissions that pollute the air. That same year, Ford also began selling TH!NK, a zero-emission electric car for urban drivers.

Ford's Bumpy Road to Success

Each year from 1986 through 2001, Ford produced 5 of the 10 best-selling vehicles in the U.S. On the eve of its 100th anniversary, faced with a financial downturn, the company refocused on improving its products. "Great products made us what we are, and they will take us where we're going," said a determined Bill Ford, chief executive officer of Ford. The statistics below compare annual net profits throughout Ford's history.

1922	$100 million	1987	$4.63 billion
1924	$82 million	1988	$5.3 billion
1949	$177 million	1991	negative $2.3 billion
1973	$870 million	1998	$22 billion
1984	$1.9 billion	2001	negative $5.45 billion
1986	$3.3 billion	2002	negative $980 million

Quality Drives Global Sales

In 2001, Ford sold 5,747,982 vehicles worldwide.

66 percent in North America	4 Percent in Asia Pacific
25 percent in Europe	1 percent in the rest of the world
4 percent in Latin America	

Source: The Ford Motor Company 2001 Annual Report

In 2003, a Ford family member—William Clay Ford—was once again in charge of the company. He proudly claimed his place in a series of ads entitled "Built to Last." These ads show him with historic photos of his great-grandfather, Henry Ford. "Ford is a great company with an incredible heritage," wrote Bill Ford in the 2001 annual report to company stockholders. "We have learned a lot in the last 100 years."

To succeed in its second century, Ford Motor Company plans to continue creating economical, safe, exciting, and high-quality products, which—like the Model T—customers simply can't resist.

More than 3.6 million Explorers have been produced since 1990

1903   Ford Motor Company is founded.

1908   The first Model T is made available to the public.

1913   The first experiments with assembly-line production begin at Ford's Highland Park plant.

1917   The first Ford truck is introduced, powered by a Model T engine.

1919   Edsel Ford succeeds his father, Henry Ford, as president. They become sole owners of the company.

1922   Ford Motor Company purchases Lincoln Motor Company for $8 million.

1927   Model T production ceases, and Model A production begins.

1932   The first Ford equipped with a V-8 engine is built.

1937   Union organizers and Ford representatives battle at the Rouge plant.

1942   World War II halts civilian car production.

1943   Edsel Ford dies. Henry Ford is re-elected president of the company.

1945   Edsel Ford's son, Henry Ford II, is named president of the company.

1947   Henry Ford dies.

1956   Ford Motor Company becomes a publicly held company, owned by stockholders.

1964   Ford introduces the Mustang, a new breed of car.

1979   Henry Ford II retires. Philip Caldwell becomes the first person outside the Ford family to lead the company.

1987   Ford designs the first car marketed world-wide, called Mondeo in Europe and Asia and Ford Contour in North America.

1999   Ford airs a television commerical around the world highlighting the company's cultural diversity.

2001   Bill Ford, Henry Ford's great-grandson, is named chief executive officer.

Bill Ford is mindful of Ford's history as he looks to the future

backers People who invest money in a business or enterprise.

bargain To negotiate and decide on the terms of an agreement. The terms state what the parties will give up and what they will receive.

chassis The framework that supports the body of an automobile.

labor contract An agreement made between employees and employers concerning wages and working conditions.

labor unions Organizations that help ensure good wages and working conditions for workers.

magneto The magnetized part of an engine that generates an electric current to start the car.

mass produce To make large quantities of a product, usually by machine.

patent An official document that states who has the right to use, make, or sell an invention.

piston A solid cylinder shaped like a soup can that fits inside the hollow cylinder of a car engine.

royalties Money paid to people who hold patents for the right to use their inventions.

shares Portions of a company that can be bought and sold by stockholders.

shock absorbers Springs installed on a vehicle to absorb rough movements and make the ride smoother.

stockholders People who pay money to own stock, or portions of a company.

strike A protest, usually against low wages or poor working conditions. When workers strike, they stop working in order to force their employer to make changes.

tinkerer A person who adjusts, repairs, and experiments. A tinkerer likes to disassemble and play with machinery and equipment.

tire tread The thick outer surface of a tire that touches the road.

turnover The number of people leaving a workplace and being replaced. A 380 percent turnover means Ford had to replace its original employees almost four times.

I N D E X

INDEX

Books

Aird, Hazel B., and Catherine Ruddiman. *Henry Ford: Young Man with Ideas*. New York: Aladdin Paperbacks, 1986.

Banham, Russ, and Paul Newman. *The Ford Century: Ford Motor Company and the Innovations that Shaped the World*. Oklahoma: Artisan, 2002.

Newton, Tom. *How Cars Work*. Vallejo, Calif.: Black Apple Press, 1999.

Weitzman, David. *Model T: How Henry Ford Built a Legend*. New York: Crown, 2002.

Web Sites

The Edsel: Information about the controversial vehicle
http://edsel.net

The Ford Motor Company official Web site
http://www.ford.com

The Henry Ford Museum and Greenfield Village
http://www.hfmgv.org

How Stuff Works
http://www.howstuffworks.com